Personal and Social Skills

A Practical Approach for the Classroom

Nigel Leech and Arthur D. Wooster

School of Education, University of Nottingham

RMEP

RELIGIOUS AND MORAL EDUCATION PRESS
A Member of the Pergamon Group of Companies

Religious and Moral Education Press
A Member of the Pergamon Group of Companies
Hennock Road, Exeter EX2 8RP

Pergamon Press Ltd
Headington Hill Hall, Oxford OX3 0BW

Pergamon Press Inc.
Maxwell House, Fairview Park, Elmsford, New York 10523

Pergamon Press Canada Ltd
Suite 104, 150 Consumers Road, Willowdale, Ontario M2J 1P9

Pergamon Press (Australia) Pty Ltd
P.O. Box 544, Potts Point, N.S.W. 2011

Pergamon Press GmbH
Hammerweg 6, D-6242 Kronberg, Federal Republic of Germany

First published 1986

Published in co-operation with the Centre for Social and
Moral Education, University of Leicester

Printed in Great Britain by A. Wheaton & Co. Ltd, Hennock Road, Exeter

ISBN 0 08-034361-9

Contents

Teaching Personal and Social Skills

Introduction

This book presents a series of activities that can be used in an educational programme to teach personal and social skills. The exercises can be used with children in the third and fourth year of the primary school, and with low-achieving children of secondary age. They are presented in an order that allows children to increase their awareness gradually. New experiences and new behaviours are difficult at first. Practice is needed, and it is necessary to move gradually from the known towards the unknown. This does not mean that the order of the exercises cannot be changed. The needs of individual children and classes differ, as does the rate of learning. However the order should be taken as a guide.

Social-skills education is about helping children become better at getting on with each other. It is impossible to define exactly what social skills are, except for particular purposes. For our purposes it is useful to think of a progressive, step-by-step movement towards more effective and satisfying communication with other people. It is more than just trying to teach children new behaviour. Such attempts are usually not very successful. Low-achieving children, in particular, will often see little relevance in the separate skills and will be unable to apply them outside the classroom.

In studies made to find out how well developmentally disabled adults have adjusted to society, one finding is dominant and consistent: their most damaging problem is a tendency to relate unsatisfactorily to other people (Goldstein 1974).

Everyone spends a large part of their time talking to, and interacting with, other people. This is especially true at school. In any school one will find children who clearly have problems in getting on with others. This is particularly unfortunate for low-achieving children, who are often very dependent on relations with peers.

Frequently the inappropriate behaviour that the children show is the product of underlying hostility and fear. The usual way to deal with this in an organization is by imposing structures and constraints which reduce to a minimum the occurrence of unsuitable actions. Rules are imposed which keep the children's behaviour within well-defined and narrow limits.

Keeping children contained and well-occupied needs a great deal of effort. Often the teacher administering this regime is left feeling frustrated, drained and dissatisfied at the end of the day. The children too are often unhappy: frustrated that their underlying problems and concerns have not been recognized. What will help is a framework of social-skills training activities flexible and comprehensive enough to give this recognition.

A Model

When trying to face the problem of inappropriate social skills and possible dissatisfaction in the classroom, it is useful to have some sort of model in mind. The model might come from a personal philosophy or it might be based on strictly practical concerns. Whatever its origins a model can help to clarify objectives and give a long-term view.

A model that has proved both practical and flexible is based on the idea of friendship. Socially skilful behaviour is typical of friends' dealings with one another. Typically, friends show that they like each other, they show each other respect, and they confide things of personal importance.

In a classroom where social skills were being learned, the teacher would expect to see these signs of increasing friendliness. From increased interaction in the training activities, the children would learn the steps which form the progressive mechanics of friendship. They would identify these steps, discuss them, and apply their learning. The expected result would be a greater liking for each other's company, an increase in voluntary co-operation, increased awareness and appreciation of the needs of others, better definition of goals, and more realistic plans for achieving them.

This model is helpful because it is a two-way one. It can be readily grasped by the children as well as the teacher. Children can understand the idea of friendship, and from their vague and rudimentary notions they can be led, step by step, to an expanded and more detailed understanding, together with the skills to use their insight to make friends. From an exploration of ways in which they are alike and ways in which they differ, they can move on to explore rules and values. This takes them to an appreciation of the ways individuals have developed their views and to an awareness of their feelings.

Children look at friendship from different perspectives. One important source of influence is the age of the child. Younger children expect friends to be 'pleasurable' (Reisman & Shorr 1978) while older ones expect them to be 'useful'. Asked what they expected of a friend, a group of children between six and fourteen years of age replied in ways that could be categorized into three groups, Bigelow (1977) thought. The youngest group sought what they personally could get from the relationship, and expressed an interest in shared activities. The next stage was one in which older children worked to set norms by establishing rules of friendship. The final stage was evident when children were able to show and express a concern for empathy, understanding and self-disclosure in the relationship. Selman (1981) also found stages a useful explanatory device, although his were not linked to age. He saw children as being at first concerned with features common to the other person and themselves; this gradually gave way to the ability to be more objective about another and tolerate differences.

Friendship offers a broad model for a programme of social-skills education. The children's own views on friendship can be used and built on through activities. Of especial use within this model is the idea of friendship developing in stages. These stages give a basic rationale for the programme. That is, at first the programme provides structures which allow the children to explore things that they have in common and to discuss the ways events relate to themselves. In the second phase the children explore rules and values, and the final phase begins the process of understanding other people's points of view and being more open with one another.

The Learning Process in Personal and Social Education

It can be said that everyone has a natural potential for learning (Rogers 1983). Clearly not everybody learns at the same rate or under the same conditions, however it is possible to list some points about the process of learning which are important for personal and social education:

1. Learning that invites the learner to see herself and others in new ways is threatening and tends to be resisted.

2. Learning that is seen as threatening is easier when other sources of threat and worry are minimized.

3. When the learner sees that the threat to self-esteem is low then learning can take place.

4. Learning is increased and becomes more significant when the learner takes an active part.

5. Learning that allows the learner to judge her own success leads to greater creativity, responsibility and self-direction.

6. Learning which is self-directed and involves the whole person of the learner – body, mind and feelings – is more useful to her.

7. To encourage real learning a wholistic approach is helpful. This means taking account of the learner's feelings. The learning needs to happen in an environment that is able to allow and contain the feelings of discomfort that go with new experience. Opportunities to express and examine different feelings are needed.

For any classroom activity to have a good chance of promoting real learning, Timmerman & Ballard (1975) suggest it must include four steps: structure, involvement, success and feedback.

Structure refers to planning, setting up and then holding to specific guidelines. This might involve just simple directions or suggesting seating arrangements. Structure provides a framework for the activity, sets limits and guides expectations, etc.

Involvement refers to participation by choice. It is a child's voluntary inclusion of herself in terms of her own personal concerns. The child, who is important in her own right, is then involved in the process of learning. She learns by doing, acting, initiating and responding. A starting structure that works well will act as a funnel, channelling the learner into the involvement stage.

Success is really a sense of satisfaction and accomplishment that comes from being involved. It might be considered self-enhancing and non-competitive. The success could simply be the total involvement that a child experiences when she is learning something that makes a difference to her. This awareness of success is the result of the child's self-evaluation of the activity.

Feedback provides some means for the child to gather information from what she did. It helps her to focus on her learning behaviour and evaluate it. This requires a degree of acceptance and a move away from the more traditional educational standpoints. These often make an outside agent the evaluator, and encourage relationships where one person wins and the rest lose. A way needs to be found to give information so that the child receiving it feels noticed and appreciated. She might then be in a better position to see what she did and how she did it. Feedback can be both descriptive and appreciative. It need not be from the teacher. Feedback can be written, given by demonstration, revealed by an expression, or spoken. When solicited by the actor from other children it is often more powerful and of more value than when volunteered by the teacher.

Trying out new ways of behaving or just receiving feedback on one's behaviour can generate feelings of discomfort and raise levels of fear. True learning necessarily involves some level of discomfort. Experiential activities can generate many different feelings which the learner may not have been fully aware of before and she may have difficulty in matching these with her heightened awareness of others. Structure and the classroom atmosphere can do much to keep these feelings within manageable limits. However, this may not be sufficient, especially since the teacher may well be experiencing new feelings herself. It is helpful to introduce techniques for relaxation into the classroom. This can act as a counterbalance to increased awareness of emotion and corresponding levels of activity.

Relaxation

Relaxation can be a new experience for children. The researchers Amerikaner and Summerlin (1982) found that learning-disabled children who were taught to relax were better able to cope with stress. Many children seem to spend much of their time in a very active state and for them just to experience some measure of relaxation must be of benefit. Schools tend to give children a lot of experience in cognitive and physical activities. Relaxation can demonstrate an alternative. Many children simply find the experience pleasurable. They often enjoy the sense of peace, and the feeling of quiet, that relaxation can produce. It is not uncommon for children to ask for more relaxation and to feel disappointed when a session is left out. Of course, some children, and adults, find relaxation difficult and the sensations produced are not always pleasant. As with other activities, it is important to avoid making the children feel compelled to take part in relaxation sessions. If given the option of joining in or not, on whatever level they choose, most children will join in. Forms of relaxation have been used with children to reduce anxiety and increase levels of thinking (Morris 1977) and to reduce hyperactivity (McBrien 1978).

5

Imagery

A natural adjunct to relaxation is the use of imagery. This is a way of encouraging children to use their imagination in a structured way. As with activities like listening to stories, guided imagery encourages children to imagine that they are elsewhere and to produce 'pictures in the head'. Imagination involves all the senses. It is not restricted to visual impressions.

Bullock & Severe (1981) found that guided visual imagery, following on directly from relaxation, was particularly useful with learning-disabled and emotionally handicapped children. They suggest that children who are more able to fantasize are better at coping with stress and are more creative.

Children spend a lot of their time using their imagination, so asking a child to use guided imagery is not asking her to do anything that she cannot already do. There is no need for the child to write thus difficulties of expression are overcome. Using imagery may allow a child to accept part of her life that she normally ignores or disallows. Alternative means of expression are made available to the child and she gets a chance to see more aspects of herself.

It is possible to use the technique to allow the class to rehearse different situations and to experience different outcomes. Children can imagine themselves succeeding or enhancing their performance in certain activities. These might range from swimming better to solving interpersonal problems on the playground. Just to experience them-selves as they would ideally like to be, in their imagination, is often very rewarding and helpful for children.

Feedback and expression of an imagined experience can be given and received in various ways. These might include talking to a partner, drawing, use of clay, models with Lego, etc. In the case of imagery work it is especially important to accept whatever is produced. Images and their representations can at times be very powerful and need to be treated with respect. Although usually pleased to have results displayed, children are sometimes uneasy with an open discussion. It is wise to respect their wishes.

Summary

A classroom that encourages real learning will be one in which there is a high level of involvement and where some activities are self-initiated and self-evaluated; and the threat to self-esteem is low. A supportive atmosphere can be enhanced by the use of relaxation and guided visual imagery. Activities that assist real learning will include the four steps of structure, involvement, success and feedback. A useful model to keep in mind is based on the idea that friendship develops in three stages. Initially children view others in terms of themselves and what they can gain from any relationship. This gives way to the formation of rules. Finally, there can be an understanding of the other person that includes an appreciation of differences.

A Programme in Three Stages

A basic premise of this programme is that children like to co-operate – they prefer to get on with each other rather than to argue and disagree. Friends are preferable to enemies. This co-operation must be brought about by the children themselves. It cannot be imposed by outside rules and values. A way to encourage this is to use a three-stage process for the development of social skills in the classroom. These stages are somewhat similar to the stages of friendship. They may be expressed as: beginning the process, examining the affective, and creating the working classroom.

Beginning the process

The starting-point is the creation of the task climate. Children will change their behaviour only when they personally see the need to do so. Change involves feelings of discomfort. Unless the classroom atmosphere can provide sufficient support to overcome and contain this unease the children are less likely to achieve change. Learners need to feel warmth and acceptance in the classroom. Differences of opinion can then be accepted, and indeed desired, as children and teachers show support for one another and become sensitive to each other's needs. Curwin & Curwin (1974) suggest that the teaching plan must be flexible enough to allow for the individual needs of children, rather than rigid, closed, and seen as more important than the children it should serve.

Children need to begin to feel comfortable. A powerful way of achieving this is to ensure that the children realize that they are not going to be forced into anything. Even when they show outward signs of agreement, people resent being forced to do things. The right to 'pass' in all activities should be made clear in action as well as words. It is important for children to know that they do not have to join in anything that they find too difficult, at that particular moment. Volunteers will take part with more enthusiasm, and, reassured, some of the more timid will join in later at their own time and pace.

Examining the affective

The affective area of living and growing includes feelings, thoughts, values, wishes and attitudes, as well as behaviour and skills. Structures can be chosen to explore values in various ways. Our value system is a central part of our make-up, shaping the way we view ourselves and others. Personal values are usually difficult to examine directly, just because they are so important. It is possible to explore these areas in fantasy and play. By learning about their own thoughts and wishes, and having those accepted by themselves and others, children can learn to value themselves, and to value others.

Increasing self-esteem develops with rising self-confidence and less energy is spent gaining the attention of others at unsuitable times. Giving and receiving feedback is an important part of the process, and helps to stabilize this growing self-esteem. It is important for a person to know how she appears to other people. It is not uncommon to be unaware of how one actually behaves. Direct confrontation concerning unskilful behaviour can be overwhelming, especially if it is with a person in authority. All it generally does is increase discomfort. Effective feedback is often indirect and may be unspoken: given, for example, through drawings or wall-charts.

Children need others to recognize and accept their uniqueness. When they have begun to be aware of an increasingly accepting and supportive atmosphere, feelings that were always below the surface can be expressed and examined. These feelings can be both positive and negative. If children are to feel able to look at feelings then it is necessary for the teacher to model acceptance, risk-taking and openness in her own behaviour.

Creating the working classroom

Some of the exercises which help the children to talk to each other, and then to examine and reflect on their style of doing so, will also introduce them to the experience of co-operation. Many will have become used to competing and accept competition as the best, perhaps the only, way to work with others. As insight grows, individuals, at different speeds and to varying degrees, will come to see how much of their own behaviour they are responsible for. As, from time to time, they experience opportunities for self-direction, they will learn the skills needed to take more responsibility for themselves.

When the chance is offered they can choose co-operation over competition or working alone. Through children working together, productivity can be increased, quality of product improved and the pleasure of a more supportive and helpful climate experienced. Both the children and their teacher are rewarded; social and academic improvement results (Kagan 1985).

During the periods given to training in social and personal skills, suitable structures can provide the learners with experience in organizing themselves to achieve a given task within an allotted time. They can learn to sort out their own discipline problems within the task group. In other periods these skills can be extended and, when it seems suitable, children can select a task which they wish to attempt, contract for time, and organize the learning group and evaluation of results. At these times the teacher is freed to facilitate learning.

Sharing knowledge is an important aspect of friendship (Ladd & Emerson 1984); friends share, and sharing makes friends. Games and structured exercises can be selected to build up co-operation and make opportunities for sharing. Work will be done more effectively when the learners have been involved in some part of the choice and trained to deal with behaviour that distracts them as it occurs and in a way which brings effective change. Sometimes it will be the teacher's behaviour which is picked out for comment and this will give an opportunity for democracy to be tried out in the class.

Summary of the three stages of the programme

1. Beginning the process
(a) Creating a classroom atmosphere that will encourage change
(b) Exploring new ways of expression and novel experience
(c) Learning more about yourself and others

2. Examining the affective
(a) Learning to value yourself and others
(b) Giving and receiving feedback
(c) Exploring and examining emotion

3. Creating the working classroom
(a) Co-operating
(b) Taking responsibility
(c) Setting and reaching realistic goals

The Teacher

The primary factor in the success of any programme is the teacher. In many ways the techniques are secondary (Wanat 1983). From this point we shall therefore address teachers directly.

It might be considered that the teacher has a three-part role in the programme. First, you would provide structure for the activities – supplying materials, organizing time, giving directions and facilitating interactions. Second, your actions and words need to support each other. It would be counterproductive to expect certain actions and ways of behaving from the children and then to behave in a different way yourself. Thirdly, you can further act as a 'good' model by joining in some of the activities. On many occasions it will be inappropriate to join in – for example, when doing so would inhibit the children. At other times it will be very appropriate and worthwhile – for example, in exercises where material is publicly displayed.

As a teacher you will have your own personal views on education and your own style of teaching. Experience has told you that certain techniques work for you. However, your style of teaching may not be creating the classroom that you want. You may feel that change is needed, but be confused and uncertain how to proceed. Your own experiences may have shown you some of the ways in which you learn. You may be aware that some of your own behaviour is not always helpful to you.

It is unreasonable to expect children to look at and possibly change their behaviour if the teacher is unwilling to examine and possibly change her own behaviour. People's fear of change allows them to go on for years using old and well-tried behaviour patterns, even if these patterns have been shown not to work well. Adults, as well as children, are often unwilling to make the changes necessary to get what they want. Unless the teacher is also prepared to experiment and make changes in her views and behaviour along with her class, activities designed to change classroom functioning will not succeed fully.

Change is unpleasant. The end result might be regarded as beneficial, but the journey towards this goal can be painful and confusing. New behaviour is often frightening just because it is novel. You will know this from your own experience. It is no less true for children, and yet teachers often unthinkingly require children to do things which produce those feelings that they themselves prefer to avoid.

The movement from old ways of behaving to new can be difficult. It is not easy to change gradually from adult-directed towards child-initiated learning. The early activities of a programme should help both the teacher and the class in this. The gradual transition then gives opportunities for both the children *and* the teacher to experience achievement. It is important for *you* to experience gains as well as for the children to do so. It is certainly true that teachers' attitudes towards themselves are more important than any techniques, practices or materials (Samuels 1977). Experience will tell you that on those days when you feel better about yourself your teaching goes better. Somebody who feels good about herself tends to be socially more skilful and to be more accepted by others. This social acceptance increases the good self-feelings. Teacher–child relationships can improve only when both parties experience significant gains, and this may influence every aspect of the social-skill learning process (Ladd & Mize 1983). A trusted, well-liked, warm and supportive adult can do much to allay children's anxieties and build self-confidence.

It is important to remember that activities do not mean the same thing to each child. It is easy to feel discouraged by negative or apathetic responses from some children. However, these are just as valid as positive, supportive responses. Even if you feel an exercise has not been successful there is a good chance that children will have gained by doing it. Changes in personal meaning and ways of relating take time, and what you might have expected the activity to produce is not always immediately apparent or may take an unusual or unexpected form. If the majority of children in a class gain nothing from a particular activity then perhaps it was not appropriate for them at that time (Curwin & Curwin 1974). If continuous and varied experiences in social activities are provided, children can begin to build new ways of behaving into their lives. When they see and experience new ways of behaving for themselves, ways that offer them personal benefit, then they can decide to make changes in their social skills that they will use outside as well as inside the classroom.

The Activities

The basis for social skills is a capacity to get on with other people. If a class is going to learn and explore new social skills that will be useful in a variety of situations then much groundwork must be done f rst. This involves developing trust and respect so that new behaviour can be tried out. A trusting, sharing and working atmosphere must be established in the classroom before real learning of social skills can take place. This takes time and careful planning. It is because this is so important that most activities in this book are devoted to building the classroom climate. Without this, social-skills education invariably fails.

A rough estimate of the time needed is given for most of the activities. This has been arrived at through doing the exercises with classes of slow-learning pupils. Obviously each class is different and the time needed for an activity will vary. The activities are set out in an order in which they could be presented to the class. There is clearly no need to stick rigidly to this, although the activities towards the end of the book tend to be more 'advanced'. Do not rush through the activities. Children need time to consolidate new information. Going too fast can cause some children undue upset and frustration. Time spent in discussion and review is time well spent. Review is particularly important and necessary. This set of activities could well occupy most of a term at three or more hours each week. Find a pace that suits both you and your class.

Getting Things Moving

Faced with a room full of people sitting down, you know you are going to have trouble getting them to move. When people arrive early for a party and sit around the room, to be joined by others as they arrive, you know your party is going to be a dull, static one. Anyone who wants to get children working together in structured situations has scmehow to get them up and moving. Public dance, party or classroom, the problem is the same.

The group has to be warmed up. You have to get the children moving in a directed way, like a footballer who rolls the ball before he kicks it since a moving ball is easier to control. One of the simplest ways is to ask the children to move the furniture. You may want the tables at the side, or the chairs in small groups; get them to do it. For added control you might ask them to move the chairs as a robot would, or a tin soldier, or anything which slows them down, or speeds them up, or keeps them quiet.

Once they are on their feet it will be easier to keep them moving and take them into the next exercise you have planned. The warm-up activity you choose should be as neutral as possible. It should call for action and no talk. Warm-ups with talk can come later, when the group is used to experiential structures. For the first few sessions give the shyest the maximum freedom whilst still trying to get them involved. The best kind of warm-up will link in with what you are going to do later, but on the first few occasions your aim will be low-threat meetings with the other class members.

You will be nervous too, with a new group, or during the first few sessions. So move. It is often a good idea always to be in the same place when you stop an activity or introduce a new one, but while the children are working you can either join in or just walk around. Avoid appearing to pry. Be ready to help those who have not heard, or not understood, but when a pair or small group have started to work you must let them get on. It may be that they are not doing what you have suggested. If possible let that be their decision. The members will be sensitive in their response to the task, and if it is too much – for some reason – for one, or all of them, they will deal with it. Perhaps they will just take longer to settle down to the task, perhaps they will spend the time on something which actually gives them the knowledge of each other and the confidence to go on. The work ethic will build up as members feel able to accept responsibility for their own learning.

Often a group who have shifted the furniture and made space to move will be nervous at the novelty. They will not know what to expect from you or what you will ask from them. It will help to free everyone if you get them to move and laugh so that tension runs away as they work together. Try standing in front of the group and saying, 'Copy me.' Lead them in a series of movements (on the spot) which develop into simple pantomime acts. If you feel it will work, add sounds. The sillier you look the better, but lead up to looking silly gradually so that the class becomes aware that everyone is doing silly things and laughing. The atmosphere will lighten, energy will build up, and everyone will have taken a little risk. Being a bit silly with each other is very cohesive, it brings the group together. In later sessions, working in pairs or trios, each child can lead in turn.

A similar activity is 'following'. In pairs, one behind the other, the follower copies the walk, gestures and actions of the leader. After

14

2 minutes each the pair talk briefly about the exercise. What makes it easier? Harder? What sorts of movement feel nice to do? When this exercise becomes familiar the group may progress to mirroring, a harder following activity in which the pair stand face to face. It is easier if they touch finger-tips and concentrate on keeping them together. Later they can be apart.

Related to this is the game of passing a face (or action). For this players form a circle, one makes a face and 'passes' that expression to her neighbour, who puts it on and, in turn, passes it to her neighbour. This can be easily linked to work on identifying and naming emotions: 'Pass a happy face', or 'You have just dropped an ice-cream. Pass that face.' The same game will allow you to work on non-verbal messages: 'You are pleased to see your friend. Pass that look', or 'You don't want to stay and talk. Pass that on.'

These exercises help observation. Creativity can be encouraged by taking an object, such as a broom, and pantomiming playing it as a guitar before passing it on. The next person changes it into something else, performs the appropriate action, and hands it on. It is possible to play this game with a lump of some imaginary plastic mass which can be patted and pushed into shape and passed on, inspected carefully, reshaped and passed on again. A further variation, with a circle of players facing the centre, is to pass a sound: with head turned to the right a member says 'Zoooom', at the same time whipping her head to the left. The player on the left, who is looking to her right, repeats the 'Zoooom', passing it to her left, and so on. This active, noisy game usually provokes laughter.

It is useful to share information about each other. This can be done by asking the children to signal agreement by shooting their hand into the air, to disagree by holding their hand down with arm straight, or to choose not to answer by folding their arms. Stand where everyone can see you and have the group arrange themselves so that they can see each other. Remind them that this exercise is to allow them to learn about each other. Ask how many of them:

Have a pet?	Wish they were older?
Can roller-skate?	Choose their own clothes?

(Remind the children to look around and check what others think.) At first it is probably best not to discuss the 'voting'. Use a few questions and pass on after each one without comment. Later the technique can be used to remind the class of attitudes to and views on certain esson topics, or the children can raise questions they wish to poll. This is a quick way to obtain feedback about the success of a lesson or activity.

If you want to get everyone up and moving around ask them to do that and give them a small task. Suggest they look at everyone as they pass and slowly shake their heads at each other; after a minute of walking round suggest that as they pass they look each other in the eye and slowly smile before moving on. Afterwards let pairs talk very briefly together about the feelings they had in the two situations. As the social-skills course goes on this exercise can be a way of revising, or examining, feelings and their physical expression. In the early stages it may be easier to start by walking around imagining a strong wind, or heavy rain, thick fog, carrying the shopping, or something of the sort. Imagining a dog under one arm and a cat under the other as they walk from one end of the room to the other can allow each person to be the focus of everyone's attention for a brief period.

Warm-ups can be used to set the tone of a lesson. Ask the children to form pairs and tell each other briefly, 'Something nice that happened to me recently', or 'Something I have that I am proud of', or 'What I would have in my room if I could build it myself.' Allow a brief exchange, basing your timing on the degree of involvement. When this activity is familiar pairs can join up to make fours. A listening exercise can be added if A explains B's earlier response, and B repeats A's. Working in pairs and fours is fairly safe and allows each member a share of someone else's attention for a brief period. Attention is essential to all of us and it helps the tone of the class to make it available to everyone in a positive and definite way.

Guided Imagery

Fantasy is concerned with imagination. A guided fantasy or guided visual imagery is simply a way of guiding imagination. Imagination deals with all the senses. A guided fantasy can encourage the use of the senses. If a child is walking along a beach, in fantasy, it is possible for her to hear the sound of the sea, to taste the salt in her mouth, to experience the smells of the seaside, to feel the wind on her face and the sand beneath her feet, as well as seeing the beach stretch out in front of her. Feelings and emotions will be associated with the experience and it is useful to ask about feelings at suitable moments in a fantasy.

Fantasy can be introduced gradually into the classroom. Quick fantasies can be used to help the class relax or prepare for a lesson or activity. For some children it is a good idea to start with eyes open. One idea is to ask the class to imagine that there is a mouse or squirrel sitting in the corner of the room. The children could describe what it is doing, move it around the room, change its colour, or bring in more animals. You could direct this fantasy or children could volunteer. Any form of story-telling is fantasy – talking, writing, drawing or art work.

A fantasy that lends itself well to the different senses involves observing a storm on a lake:

> Imagine that you are standing at the edge of a large lake ... There is a big storm ... The wind is howling, and the rain is falling ... There is thunder and lightning ... You can hear the wind and the thunder ... feel the rain on your face ... perhaps you can even taste it in your mouth ... Out on the lake is a small boat ... It is being tossed and thrown about by the storm ... Watch the boat ... The lake is full of large waves and the sky is black with rain ... As you watch, the storm gradually begins to calm ... Slowly the black clouds clear and the wind begins to die down ... The rain becomes less ... The noises of the storm get less ... The sun comes out through the clouds ... The sky clears ... It is a bright blue ... The lake is smooth and calm and the boat floats gently on its surface ... Feel the warmth of the sun on your face ... Perhaps you can hear the birds as they fly in the sunlight ... Smell the grass and flowers as they dry out in the calm after the storm ... Listen to the sounds around you and smell the smells as you watch the boat floating on the flat surface of the lake in this calm place ... Spend a few moments enjoying the peace and calm ... When you are ready open your eyes and perhaps have a stretch.

Other fantasies might include children imagining that they are:

> a balloon floating gently through the sky,
> a snowman melting in the warm sun,
> a seagull soaring above the sea,
> a cat lying in front of a fire, stretching as it wakes up,
> sitting on a river bank watching the river slowly flow by, feeling the cool water as they dangle their feet in it.

Always use as many senses as possible.

Be creative. Make up your own fantasies to suit the situation Treat the children's experiences with respect. Do not interpret. Listen!

Relax! Relax!

There are various techniques for relaxation training that can be used in the classroom. The method that you find the simplest is probably the best. Do not be afraid to vary or add any instructions to suit your own style and pace, and those of your class.

Some children seem to be unaware of the difference between relaxation and tension. One way to introduce children to the idea of relaxation is to spend some time observing the difference between tensed and untensed muscles. With a hand placed on a large muscle group it is possible to feel the difference.

Get the children to feel their biceps while they make them as tense as possible and then relax. Notice the difference. Forearms can be tensed by making a tight fist. If you sit upright in a chair and try to push your heels into the floor the large muscles of your thighs will tighten. This muscle movement can usually be clearly seen. Demonstrate with your own muscles.

Children can experience relaxation by tensing all their muscles as tightly as they can (including screwing up their faces) and then quickly letting the tension go, perhaps with a sound. Repeat two or three times.

Relax along with your class. Talk about relaxation as opposed to tension. What causes stress in school? Do any of your class find that relaxation practice helps them outside your lessons?

Children can relax well lying forward on their desks with head on hands (children who wear glasses should remove them). It is a good idea to let children know that they do not have to join in if they do not want to, although they must remain quiet and still so as not to disturb those who do want to relax. You might use a relaxation sequence like the following, pausing where appropriate:

> Take a couple of deep breaths and begin to relax ... begin to let the tension go ... Most people find it easier to relax with their eyes closed ... If you want to peep then that's fine ... Take your attention to your feet ... Allow your feet to begin to relax ... Let the tension slowly seep away ... Imagine your feet becoming warm and heavy ... warm and heavy as they become more relaxed ... Let this feeling of warmth and heaviness in your feet begin to creep up your legs ... up past your ankles and then your knees as you let your legs become relaxed ... warm and heavy ... Both your legs feeling warm and heavy ... This feeling of warmth and heaviness creeps up past your bottom, up to your stomach and lower back

... warm and heavy as you let more of the tension go ... up to the top part of your back and your chest ... right up to your shoulders ... Let those muscles in your shoulders relax ... warm and heavy ... Perhaps you want to move them slightly as the tension seeps away ... warm and heavy ... Let this feeling of relaxation in your shoulders flow down your arms ... down past your elbows, past your wrists and down into your hands ... right down to the tips of your fingers ... Maybe your hands feel a bit tingly as a sign that you are becoming very relaxed ... If they don't then that doesn't matter, you can still be very relaxed ... deep relaxation in your hands ... warm and heavy ... Let this relaxation that's in your hands flow back up your arms ... up past your elbows to your shoulders and up the back of your neck ... Let those muscles in your neck relax ... warm and heavy ... Imagine this warmth and heaviness going up over the top of your head and flowing down over your face ... It flows down over your face ... Feel the muscles of your face smooth out as they become more relaxed ... As you let the tension go out of your face you can feel your face becoming smooth and relaxed ... Stay feeling calm and relaxed for a few moments ... warm, heavy and relaxed ... You can keep this calmness and relaxation all day ... You can come back to it whenever you want to ... Now begin to come back to this room ... You can slowly become more alert, more awake, but staying relaxed and calm ... When you are ready open your eyes ... Perhaps have a stretch ... like a cat.

If certain children do not seem to want to open their eyes straight away that does not matter. A touch on the shoulder, stroke on the back of the neck or gentle shake is usually sufficient. Sometimes a child will be fast asleep. This could simply mean that the child needs a sleep and it may be appropriate to let her sleep quietly for a while. It is not necessary for a child to be lying forward on her desk with her eyes closed in order for her to relax. A child who is sitting up with eyes open and looking around can still be working and participating in the session. A child's seeming restlessness may in fact be an indication of an increase in awareness. The children may be working hard to make sense of relationships in the classroom.

A useful display for relaxation training is a large outline of the human figure. The parts of the body mentioned in the relaxation sequence can be clearly labelled.

The Planet

This is an idea for using extended guided visual imagery. It provides the class with a chance to experience a sense of deep relaxation and to use their imagination more fully than they might normally do.

Time   20 to 30 minutes, maybe longer.

Materials   None.

Procedure   After the class have settled and are fairly deeply relaxed, following an appropriate relaxation sequence, take them through the following guided fantasy:

> Imagine yourself climbing into a car that is going to take you to the launching pad of a spaceship ... You are driving along the road ... The car stops and you get out ... In front of you is the launching pad ... Standing on the launching pad is a spaceship ... It is your spaceship ... Have a look at your spaceship ... What size and shape is it? ... What colour is it? ... Walk round it ... As you walk round it you see the steps leading up to the door of the spaceship ... Climb the steps and enter your spaceship ... Have a look round inside ... What is it like inside? ... What can you see? ... What does it feel like? ... What does it smell like? ... Sit down in the pilot's seat and look at the controls in front of you ... The spaceship is about to take off ... You are going to fly it ... Work the controls ... The engine starts and the spaceship begins to lift off the launch pad ... It rises higher and higher, faster and faster until it leaves the earth behind and is flying through space ... Your spaceship is flying through space with you at the controls ... What is it like in space? ... What does it feel like flying through space? ... Look out of the windows of your spaceship ... You are beginning to approach a planet ... You come closer to this planet and you get ready to bring your spaceship in to land ... Carefully you bring your spaceship down and land it on the planet ... You go outside ... Have a look round this strange planet ... See what you can find ... Are there any people there or strange beings? ... What are the rocks like? ... What are the plants like? ... Are they strange? ... Are there any animals there? ... What does it feel like? ... What does it smell like? ... Are there any sounds that you can hear? ... Spend some time exploring this planet ... Have a good look round ... Hidden somewhere on this planet is a bottle of magic liquid ... Look for this

magic bottle ... Look around the planet ... Suddenly you realize that you know where this bottle is hidden ... You know where the magic bottle is ... Go there and get the magic bottle ... Where is this place? ... What does the bottle look like? ... If you drink this magic liquid you know that it will make you feel calm and relaxed, really O.K. about yourself ... really good ... You can take th s bottle with you and drink from it whenever you want to ... Take the bottle of magic liquid and go back to your spaceship ... Get ready for take-off ... Take off and leave the planet ... You are flying through space ... You are approaching earth ... You bring your spaceship in to land ... It lands back at the launching pad ... With your bottle of magic liquid, if you want it, climb into the car and drive back to this room ... back to this classroom ... When you are ready open your eyes and perhaps have a stretch.

Note   Give the children a chance to share their experiences in some way. Suggesting that they tell their neighbour about their planet and magic bottle might well be sufficient.

Brainstorming

Brainstorming is a creative technique for generating ideas and suggestions on a particular subject. It gives children the opportunity to be valued and accepted in a non-critical way. Any topic can be used for a brainstorm: for example, 'things we do in school' or 'uses of a chair'. Children simply call out ideas as fast as they can and the teacher writes them on the blackboard or a large sheet of paper exactly as they are said. There are no 'turns'; anyone calls out whenever they have an idea. Anyone can follow on from anyone else's idea. The rules are that no one makes any comment or criticism whatsoever about any idea and that every suggestion is written down as it is without comment. Ideas need to be kept short – a single word or phrase. Do not write them in a list, but jumble them up all over the blackboard. A list implies that the top item is the most important. Make sure that the topic or heading is clear and that everybody understands exactly what it means before you start. Use this activity at fairly regular intervals.

Grouping

It is possible to reduce the number of items generated by a brainstorm quite quickly, to be left with the key items or concerns of the class at that particular time. This is done by quickly going through all items in turn and asking all those who wish the item to be retained to put their hand up. Write the number of votes next to each item. Remove those with a small number of votes and rub out the numbers beside the items to be retained. Repeat until you are left with the required number of items. A child can vote for any number of items and can change her vote between voting sessions. Make sure that all the class agree on those items to be deleted.

What Have I Done?

This gives children the chance to be listened to and accepted by at least one other person, and to practise listening to others.

Time   Approximately 20 minutes.

Materials   None.

Procedure   Ask the children to form pairs sitting facing each other and to decide who is A and who is B. Child A starts and tells B all the things that she can remember doing between leaving school yesterday and arriving at school this morning. Child B's task is to listen to A as carefully as she can, asking questions if she wishes. After 3 minutes A and B swap round for a further 3 minutes.

Now each pair finds another pair to work with so that the class is in groups of four. They spend about 4 minutes comparing what they have been talking about.

The activity is finished off by forming everybody into a large circle and asking them to mention some of the things that they have been talking about and to say how they felt about the activity, if they want to.

Note   There might well be other, more relevant topics that the class could explore using this discussion style. If any of the pairs or groups appear to be in difficulty or remain silent then it is an important part of the activity to allow them to experience this.

Think Up a Game

This has children working together in groups and receiving praise from others. It can be used to extend a warm-up activity, or can be just fun.

Time   30 minutes plus.

Materials   None.

Procedure   The children form groups of four and are given no more than 5 minutes to think up a game to teach to the rest of the class. The game must be one that can be played in the classroom. Each group in turn then teaches their game to the rest of the class. Allow time for each game to be played by the class and make a point of encouraging each group by getting the class to clap, or thank them in some way, after they have 'given' their game.

Note   Accept any reasonable game, including games that may already be well known to the class. The quality of the game does not matter, the aim is to encourage participation and appreciation.

Name Draw

This allows children to acknowledge another publicly, and helps to increase self-esteem.

Time 5–10 minutes. This is a handy quick activity that can be used at various times during the day, or week, etc.

Materials Card, small box or bag.

Procedure Write each child's name on a separate piece of card and place the cards in the box or bag. Draw two names out of the 'hat', e.g. A and B. Then ask A to make a particular type of statement about B. This could range from simply something about B's clothing or looks that A likes to a much more affirming comment such as how B has helped A. Repeat with two more names.

Note It is useful to stop this exercise after a few goes and repeat it at a later date rather than continuing until everybody has had a turn. Depending on what the class is concerned with, it is possible to vary the type of statement: for example, you could ask, 'A, tell us what makes B a good friend', or 'How has B helped you this week?'

People Like Me

This is a very good activity to use early on in a programme. It enhances self-esteem and gives children practice in making positive statements.

Time   1 hour plus.

Materials   Pencils, crayons, plain paper and an index card or lined paper of similar size for each child.

Procedure   Write each child's name down the left-hand side of the blackboard. Draw a line across the board under each name. Start with the first child on the list and ask her to pick two children in the class whom she likes. Ask these two children to stand up one at a time and say what they like about the child who picked them. If there is difficulty then you can prompt by suggesting that they might say something that she is good at (e.g. swimming, writing, etc.). Insist that the statements are positive. Write the statements next to the child's name. Any statement that seems doubtful can be checked with the child to see if she will accept it as a positive statement about herself. Repeat with each child in the class. Include yourself if the class want it. This gives you the chance to pick children who might have been left out.

Have each child copy the statements that are next to her name on to an index card or paper.

Everybody then draws a picture of themself and fixes their card to the picture. Mount the pictures on the wall. Do not forget to include your own.

About Me!

This helps to clarify values and gives an opportunity to value and accept others. It encourages self-expression.

Time   Approximately 30 minutes.

Materials   Enough 'About me' sheets for everyone; pens or pencils.

Procedure   Make up the 'About me' sheets. These consist of a short list of sentence stems, such as:

My name is ....

I like ....

I am happy doing ....

More than anything else I like ....

If I had to have another name I would like to be called ....

I get sad when...

Two people who have made me cry are ....

When I get angry I feel ....

Something I would like people to say about me is ....

I would like someone to give me...

Signed ....

Everybody fills in their own sheet. Go through the sentences one at a time so that all the children can keep up. Accept whatever the children want to say and write difficult words on the blackboard. Provide model answers by giving examples about yourself (e.g. tell the class what makes you sad). Fill in your own sheet. You may like the children to colour or draw on their sheets to make them more personal. Display the sheets so that the class can spend time looking at each other's answers.

Note   Make up your own sentence stems or get the children to suggest them, and repeat the activity on another occasion. Always use positive sentence stems. Do not judge the children's work.

In the Circle

This is designed to help classroom discussions. It allows children to speak and be listened to without interruption. This activity works best if held regularly.

Time   Allow about 30 minutes. Be fairly strict about this.

Materials   Beanbag or similar object.

Procedure   Decide beforehand on a topic for discussion. In early sessions the topics should be very 'non-threatening'. They might include such ideas as 'watching television', 'what we did over the weekend' or reviewing previous activities. Later, as the class gains more confidence, the topics can gradually become more 'personal'. At times the class might simply want to talk or use the time to explore current concerns.

Explain the rules for the discussion. These are that everybody gives the speaker their full attention and only the person holding the beanbag is allowed to speak. If anybody wants to say anything they must wait until the speaker has finished and has passed them the beanbag.

Note   It is important for the teacher to abide strictly by the rules as well. Allow children plenty of time to get used to this activity. You may well find it necessary to remind the class of the task: that is, to discuss the topic. Be patient with children who find this difficult and do not intervene too much. If you are going to include this activity use it at least once a week.

Friends

This gives the class a chance to explore the idea of friendship and to begin looking at relationships and feelings that exist in the class.

Time   Approximately 1 hour.

Materials   None.

Procedure   Begin by spending some minutes talking with the class about friendship. Discuss such things as getting on with other people, who is a friend, and what makes a friend. Accept whatever responses the children give and encourage them to talk. There is no need to spend long on this. Bring the discussion to a close and settle the class down for some relaxation.

Give the class a short relaxation followed by a guided fantansy about meeting their ideal friend. Have them imagine themselves with their ideal friend. This friend could be somebody that they actually know, somebody that they would like to know, or somebody completely fictitious. Ask them to imagine:

> Who is your friend? ... What sex are they? ... How old? ... Where are you? ... What are you doing? ... What are you talking about?

When you have finished the fantasy get the children to form pairs and talk about their ideal friend (5 minutes). Then each pair can find another pair to work with so that the class is in groups of four. In these fours they can share their experience of the fantasy and talk about friendship (6 minutes).

Now get the class into a large circle to talk about what has just happened. After any discussion brainstorm around 'friendship', writing all words and comments on the blackboard as they are said. Then vote to find three central notions about friendship that concern the class at that particular moment. You may want to display the results of the brainstorm and voting. Allow any discussion that might develop.

Note   Allow any feelings that arise to be openly discussed, if the children want to. Do not be tempted to break into any silences that may develop in the small groups. If some children find parts of this exercise difficult, respect their silences or giggles. It can be useful to have a child acting as an observer who sits out of the activities and then comments on how particular groups have behaved. She could report back to the large circle.

Keep Out

In this activity children can experience being ignored by a group. They can also practise working with others on a task and experience acceptance by others.

Time   Approximately 20 minutes.

Materials   None.

Procedure   Form the class into groups of about six. One child from each group goes outside (or to another part of the classroom) and the others sit in a tight circle. Give the groups a topic that they will find easy to talk about (e.g. swimming). The children who went outside then come in to tell their group about a present that they have just received or something that has happened to them. The children will probably need to be told what to talk about and it has to be something important to them. They must try and interest their group in this important topic, whilst the task of the groups is to ignore them completely and talk about the group topic. After 2 minutes stop and have the groups re-admit the 'outsider'. Allow each child who wants to to have a go at being the outsider.

Note   It may be necessary occasionally to remind the class that the task of the groups is to *ignore completely* the person wishing to join them and then to welcome her back into the group. Do not force any child to have a go at being the outsider. You may well find that the majority of the class do not want to be on the outside.

I Would Rather Be ...

This encourages the clarification of values and helps to enhance self-concept.

Time Approximately 20 minutes.

Materials Enough 'I would rather be ...' sheets for everybody, pencils.

Procedure Make up a worksheet using about a dozen pairs of words, or short phrases, like this:

I Would Rather Be ...
Which would you prefer to be out of each of these pairs?

1. cat ....dog
2. rich ....poor
3. rich ....beautiful
4. happy.......................................sad
5. alone ....with other people
6. horse ....sheep
7. bat ....ball
8. tree ....flower
9. left...right
10. apple ....banana
11. dog...wolf
12. river ....sea

Give each child a sheet. Read the sheet out to the class then go through it with them line by line, having instructed them to circle the options they would prefer. This means that you can check on those children who have difficulty with reading and you can keep reminding the class of the precise task, i.e. if they *were* a cat or a dog, which one would they rather *be*? When they have finished, ask the children to walk around the classroom and see if they can find anyone who has circled the same choices. Allow any discussion that might develop. Display the sheets.

Note Make up your own pairs of words; these might be applicable to current classroom concerns. Fill in a sheet yourself.

Helping Each Other

This allows children to say publicly who in the class has helped them and in what way.

Time   Approximately 30 minutes initially. The chart can be used over a number of weeks.

Materials   Large sheet of paper or card for a wall-chart; large supply of small pieces of card (about 5 cm by 5 cm); one small envelope for each child; pens and pencils; map pins.

Procedure   Spend a few minutes discussing with the class how they help each other in the classroom. Ask them what they actually do to help each other. Stop when you have three specific ways which the class agree with. Write these on the blackboard.

Give each child ten small cards and get them to write their name on each one. Divide the wall-chart into three columns and write one of the 'ways to help' at the bottom of each column. Put the chart on the wall. Write the name of each child on an envelope and fasten each envelope near to the wall-chart.

Explain to the class that whenever anyone in the class helps them in one of the three ways, they can show this by pinning the helper's name in the appropriate column. Their name cards will be kept in their envelope on the wall. Put the cards into the envelopes. Ask if anyone wants to pin up someone's name.

Note   Remind the class about the chart regularly and about helping each other in the classroom. Congratulate children for having their name put on the chart.

Go Away!

This is another version of 'Keep out', although the aims are slightly different. Here each child can experience some rejection followed by acceptance from the class. The activity can be used to increase class feelings of 'unity' and self-esteem through group acceptance. It allows those children who might not normally do so to experience some 'safe' rejection by others.

Time   30 minutes plus.

Materials   None.

Procedure   Start off with one volunteer and arrange the rest of the class, including yourself, in a tight circle sitting in chairs and facing inwards. The child on the outside then walks round the circle asking whoever she wants to let her in. The child who is asked either ignores her or tells her to go away. After a short while (perhaps less than a minute) tell the child on the outside that the next person she asks will let her in. She can choose who to ask. Instruct the person chosen to invite her in warmly. The class could clap her. Allow whoever wants to to have a go on the outside.

Note   This exercise can involve a lot of feeling. You might well find that the whole class wants a go. Make sure that you include yourself. Do not be afraid to dramatize the acceptance back into the class group. This can have a powerful effect on a child's self-esteem.

How Not to Listen

This can demonstrate dramatically the action of ignoring someone, and illustrates ineffective communication skills. It gives some children the chance to achieve group recognition.

Time   20 minutes plus.

Materials   None.

Procedure   Seat the children in a semicircle. Ask for two volunteers and explain that you are going to do a short drama or play. You take the role of a teacher, one of the children plays a child whose work you are looking at and the other child is to come in with an urgent message for the teacher (e.g. accident on playground). When the messenger approaches you make a point of turning your back on her. Do this, with obvious exaggerated movements, two or three times while the child keeps trying to get your attention. Stop and ask the class what you did. Repeat two or three times with other children acting the roles. Get the children to decide who is going to play which part and make sure that they have the opportunity to take the role of teacher with you taking another role.

Note   Do not force any child to take a role if she does not want to. Only a few children may want to take part. When asking what happened accept anything to do with blocking or ignoring. Finish off with a discussion about listening skills.

When I Wasn't Listened To

This gives children the chance to explore and talk about times when they were ignored. It encourages acceptance and gives practice in listening skills.

Time Approximately 1 hour.

Materials None.

Procedure Split the class into groups of four. Each group is then to spend 5 minutes thinking up a situation in which someone is not listened to or not understood. They must practise so that they can show this situation to the rest of the class as a short play. Let the children decide in which order they want the groups to perform. Accept what each group has to offer and have the rest of the class applaud after each performance.

The class now divides into threes to discuss actual situations when they have been ignored or not listened to. Give examples, if necessary, to get them started (e.g. 'Maybe your mum doesn't listen to you sometimes when you want to do or say something', or 'Brothers and sisters often don't listen to people'). Allow 5 minutes for this.

Have the class sit in a circle to discuss what they have just done. After talking about ignoring, shift the discussion to considering how people might listen to each other. How can you show that you are listening or being listened to? Accept and encourage comments, writing them on the blackboard (as in a brainstorm). If possible divide the comments into three groups – how your face looks, how your body looks, and what you say. Talk about and demonstrate these three important listening skills.

Note Whilst not being afraid to give examples to get the class started, do not be tempted to rush in quickly if any person or group seems to be having difficulty. Silences can be part of the learning process. Remind the class of these basic listening skills as occasions arise during classroom or other activities. Assist the children to listen to each other whenever, and however, you can.

Tribes

This helps the class to explore feelings.

Time   30 minutes plus.

Materials   Four pictures showing respectively an angry, a sad, a happy and a frightened face.

Procedure   Divide the class into four groups. Explain that each group is a tribe on an island, and that each tribe can feel and act in only one way. Give a picture to each group, so that one group represents the 'angry tribe', one the 'sad tribe', etc. Each group then spends 5 minutes thinking and talking about their 'tribe feeling', and how they have been made to feel like that. At the end of the 5 minutes tell them that they have another 5 minutes to work out a short play about their feeling to show to the rest of the class. Each group then demonstrates their feeling to the rest of the class. If they want to, let the groups change their feeling and do another play about the new feeling. Stop while interest is still high and finish with a class discussion in a large circle.

Note   Accept all group demonstrations. It is often useful to retell the story of the drama when a group has finished. A group's lack of acting ability can leave the rest of the class a little confused. Retelling the story helps to clarify, demonstrates that you have been interested and reduces embarrassment. Have the class clap after each demonstration and thank the group.

I Am Good. I Am Kind. I Am O.K.

This demonstrates how you can be hurt or put down by what people say.

Time   Approximately 20 minutes plus use throughout the day.

Materials   A piece of paper or card (approximately 12 cm by 20 cm) for everybody, and string so that it can be hung around the neck; pencils and crayons.

Procedure   Choose a name that no one in the class has (e.g. Ralph), and say that you are going to tell the class about a day in the life of a boy named Ralph who is the same age as they are: give an appropriate age. Explain that every morning Ralph wakes up feeling that he is good, kind and O.K. Every morning he thinks to himself, 'I am good. I am kind. I am O.K.' On the blackboard write clearly 'I am good. I am kind. I am O.K.' and read it through with the children a couple of times. Also write it clearly on a piece of paper or card.

Then go through a day in the life of Ralph. Make his day as much like a day that the children in your class would experience as possible, including time at school. Throughout the day, from getting up to going to bed, Ralph is hurt by others through no fault of his own. His mother shouts at him, his brothers bully him, he misses the school bus and he is continually picked on at school, etc. Every time Ralph is hurt like this, tear off a piece of the card on which you have written 'I am good. I am kind. I am O.K.' so that the class knows that each time a bit of his good feelings about himself disappears. By the time he goes to sleep the whole card has disappeared.

Children often find this very moving. It is possible to continue the exercise in one or more ways:

(a) Split the children into groups of three to discuss similar things that have happened to them. The class could then form a large circle for a more open discussion if that seems appropriate.

(b) The class could make up their own story, adding their own events and ideas. As each child volunteers something that is hurtful you tear another piece off an 'I am good. I am kind. I am O.K.' card.

(c) The children could each make their own card clearly labelled 'I am good. I am kind. I am O.K.' They could decorate these cards to make them more personal. The cards are then hung around their necks so that whenever they feel that someone has done anything to hurt them they tear a piece off. This could be continued throughout the day. Make sure that you wear a card as well. It would seem reasonable to remove the cards at break times.

Voting

This encourages group participation and helps to demonstrate common concerns.

Time 15 minutes.

Materials None.

Procedure First instruct the class how to register their vote: thumbs up for 'yes', thumbs down for 'no' and arms folded for 'don't know'. You then ask the class a series of questions and they respond by voting. Join in the voting yourself.

You could start by asking:

'How many of you like teachers?'
(Expected response: majority vote negative.)
'How many of you like a particular teacher?'
(Expected response: majority vote positive.)

This introduction allows you to see if the children are discriminating in their response. Alternatives can be used: for example,

'Who likes school?'
'Who likes to stay up late?'
'Who has a pet?'
'Who likes to go out with friends?'
'Who has nightmares sometimes?'

Note Keep the list of questions short. This exercise seems to appeal more to younger children than to older children. Be careful not to use it to get information unfairly. Make sure that the children look round and gather the information being offered.

Presents

This encourages valuing and giving. It can generate a lot of feeling especially amongst children who are not used to giving anything to or receiving anything from each other.

Time   30 minutes plus.

Materials   Pencils and crayons; three cards approximately 15 cm by 10 cm and three small pieces of card for each child; small box or bag.

Procedure   Write each child's name on three small pieces of card and place them in the box. Draw three cards out of the 'hat'. Make sure the names on the cards are different; if not, replace one duplicate and draw again. Give the three cards to one of the children whose name has been drawn out. Repeat until each child has three cards, one of which has her name on it.

   Hand out the larger cards and crayons. Each child is now going to give three presents: one to herself and two to the other children whose name cards she has. The presents are drawn on the larger cards, which are then folded and the recipient's name written on. When everyone has finished, the 'presents' are put into the box, shuffled and handed out. Everyone gets three presents, one from herself.

Note   Encourage children to use their imagination to give wildly extravagant presents that they think the other person would like. If necessary it is possible to ensure that children do not get the names of anyone to whom they are likely to give an unpleasant present. Allow any discussion that may develop.

Special Place

This creates working groups. It encourages group co-operation and gives experience of decision-making in a group.

Time 1 hour plus.

Materials Pencils and crayons; a piece of card and large sheet of paper for each group.

Procedure Divide the class into groups of four. Give the children time to get together with people that they want to work with. Insist that they take trouble to choose the group that they join since they might be together for some time. Allow them to solve this on their own as part of the learning process. Each group sits around a table, and has a card, paper and crayons. They choose a name for their group and write it on the card.

Give the class a relaxation exercise and guided fantasy. Take time with the relaxation to ensure that everybody is fairly well relaxed. Then go into the guided fantasy. Tell the class that they are going on a special journey to a special place. They are travelling in their groups and so will be with their friends. Quickly take them on the journey. They may need to decide what to bring and how to travel. Spend time at the special place. Here they can do what they want and have what they want. They are with their friends. Take time to look around. Ask such questions as: 'What is the place like?', 'Where is it?', 'What are your friends like?', 'What are they doing?', 'How do you feel in this special place?'

Bring the children back to the classroom. Encourage silence and ask each four to make a group drawing of the special place. Each person in the group contributes. Encourage children to draw at the same time, and extend each other's work. Allow the children to experience the problems of working in a group. When they have finished, the pictures and group names can be displayed.

Note It is a good idea to keep these groups as work groups for future activities. A similar process to this can be used to create other work groups for 'academic' subjects.

Using Clay

This creative use of clay enables groups to work together on a task. It encourages a group identity with sharing and valuing. As well as gaining pleasure and satisfaction from handling clay, the class can review work and progress using an alternative medium.

Time   1 hour plus.

Materials   Clay, boards and tools for working the clay; newspaper for covering tables, etc.; water; overalls, towels, etc.

Procedure   Ask the children to divide into work groups. Each group sits around a table and is supplied with clay, tools and a small amount of water. Take the class through a relaxation and short guided fantasy to remind them of previous work and activities that they have done in the programme. Get them to review their work from various angles, in their imagination. Tell them that each group is going to work together to make a model out of clay to show people some of the things that they have been doing. They might imagine that it is for a group of children from another school. Get them to start slowly and gradually working the clay. Encourage them to work quite silently and together, so that each group produces one model. Allow the activity to last as long as the class seems to want.

Note   Resist the temptation to intervene when a group seems stuck. Sorting out group problems is a part of the learning process. Just handling clay seems to be an important experience for some children. Allow children to indulge in the tactile pleasures of using clay. The production of a model is secondary to the group experience.

Giving Colours

This encourages giving. It also allows children to express feelings and thoughts to each other in a non-verbal way. Some children can receive strong messages about how others in the class see them. It is possible for children to gain much from this activity.

Time   Approximately 20 minutes initially. This is an on-going activity that children add to at other times.

Materials   Large wall-chart divided into columns with a child's name at the foot of each column; plenty of small squares of card in two distinct colours, e.g. grey and yellow, of a size that fits on the columns of the wall-chart; map pins.

Procedure   Talk with the children about how colours can be used to express various ideas or feelings: for example, 'a grey day', 'red hot', 'feeling blue' and 'in the pink'. Give each child two cards, one of each colour. Suggest that the cards might mean different things. The yellow card could mean something different from the grey card. The yellow might stand for a 'positive' or 'warm' feeling about someone, and the grey a 'negative' or 'cool' feeling. Do not make a clear explanation of this to the children; that might interfere with the depth and personal content of the activity. Allow them to reach personal decisions. You can simply suggest that the cards might mean different things and reinforce this by, for example, saying that children could regard the yellow card as being 'golden'. Here 'golden' does not just describe the card's colour, but also provides a 'feeling attribute'.

The children then give their cards to each other, with the proviso that both cards cannot be given to the same person. If it seems appropriate, allow the class a few moments to talk and compare after they have done this. They then pin the cards they have received on to the wall-chart above their name.

Make sure that there is a supply of cards and pins available so that anyone can give another card whenever they want to, by pinning one above someone's name. Draw the attention of the class to the chart at least once a day. Remind them that the chart is a way of giving or saying things to each other.

Note   There is no need to suggest meanings for the colours of the cards; just stress that different colours might stand for different things. After a few days you might well find that patterns are emerging.

Comment on this. Clearly a child who has very few cards compared with others is being told something by the class, as are children receiving far more than others. Mentioning this might be useful, but remember not to imply criticism. You could simply ask the child how she feels about it. The chart may be saying more about the class as a whole than about individual members.

I Feel ...

This allows children to work in groups towards the goal of sharing and stating feelings to each other. The class can increase their understanding of each other's feelings.

Time   40 minutes to 1 hour.

Materials   Pens and pencils; about 30 small index cards and at least two 'I feel ...' sheets for each child; a card headed 'Feelings we like' and a card headed 'Feelings we don't like' for each work group (with about four members).

Procedure   Spend a few minutes brainstorming the class around the notions 'how we can feel' or 'I feel ...', so that you end up with between 15 and 25 'feeling words' on the blackboard. Split the class into work groups of about four. Divide the blank index cards amongst the groups and instruct them to write each 'feeling word' that they have just brainstormed on a separate card. The groups should each end up with a pile of 'feeling words' and some blank cards. Let each group sort out how it is going to achieve this task.

When they have all finished give each group a 'Feelings we like' and a 'Feelings we don't like' card, and have them sort the other cards into two piles under those headings. When they have completed this have them put each pile in order of liking or disliking, respectively. If they want to add any more words they can use the blank cards. This way each group ends up with the feeling that they like the most at the top of one pile and the feeling that they like the least at the top of the other. It might well be found that each group has the same feelings at the top. If they do not, you might want the class to decide which two feelings to keep as the class 'most liked' and 'least liked'.

Give everybody two 'I feel ...' sheets. Ask them to write the most liked feeling word on one sheet and the least liked on the other then draw expressions on the faces to correspond to the feelings. Explain that they are going to give these sheets to other children in their group and that the task of the group is to ensure that everyone has filled in the rest of their sheets. You can encourage them to help each other. When the sheets have been completed and signed the children give them to other members of the group.

Note   Allow time for any discussion that might develop: comparing sheets, etc. Display the sheets if the class wish to do so.

46

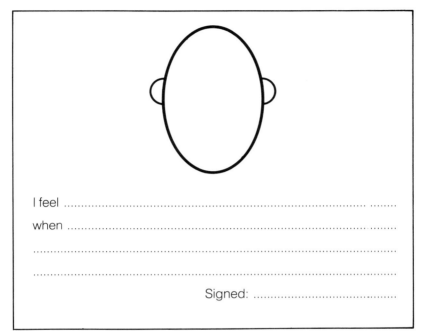

I feel ....

when ....

....

....

Signed: ....

47

I Felt ... When ...

Dear ....

  I felt ....

when you ....

....

....

                         Signed: ....

This helps children to express their feelings to each other and to make specific comments about another's behaviour.

Time   30 minutes plus.

Materials   Large supply of 'I felt ... when ...' cards, each approximately 6 cm by 6 cm; large wall-chart divided into columns with a child's name at the bottom of each column; pencils; map pins.

Procedure   Spend some minutes talking about feelings and how we often allow ourselves to feel 'good' or 'bad' depending on other people's actions. Perhaps remind the class of previous activities in this area. Have a list or chart showing different feelings. Either use one obtained in a previous exercise or brainstorm. Form the class into work groups of four each sitting around a table.

Give everybody two 'I felt ... when' cards. Explain that they are going to fill in the cards and give them to two people in their group. Spend time making sure that everyone understands and insist that they can address each card only to someone in their group (this helps reduce tension). Accept whatever the children produce and help anyone in difficulty. Encourage children to help others in their group.

Tell the children to swap cards. Each person then pins the cards they have received above their name on the wall-chart. Do this in groups.

Have a supply of cards and pins so that anyone can fill in a card and pin it above someone's name whenever they want to. Probably not all the class will do this.

48

Note You may want to use this exercise as an addition to the activities 'Giving colours' and 'I feel ...'. In the first case you will need 'I felt ... when ...' cards in the two colours, and in the second to group the feelings.

If you do decide to do these in combination then you will need to exercise some caution. These activities involve the expression of feelings, often hidden or previously unspoken. It is unwise to expose feelings too early. A group needs time to develop the kind of atmosphere and climate where participants feel secure enough to explore what can be difficult emotions. Done too early this can cause not only unwanted discomfort, but also withdrawal, loss of interest and hostility from the children. You, as the teacher and facilitator of the class group, could find yourself having to face uncertainty and confusion in the children, as well as doubts and feelings in yourself that you may be unprepared for.

It is best to regard the 'I felt ... when ...' activity as advanced.

Afterword

Now that you have read the book what are your feelings? It is important that you do not disregard your feelings and the thoughts which arise as you imagine yourself trying out the exercises with your class. Personal and social education must deal with the emotions and most of us, as adults, have learned to control these very firmly; we do not relish the thought of reviewing our emotional life, even at second hand through the struggles of others.

Children's ability to relate to others is too important to overlook. It is generally assumed that they will pick up enough skills to get by in life. A little informal teaching, the odd comment, is often assumed to be enough to introduce them to ways to get along in our society. But this is not enough for many children, and especially slow-learning children. Their lack of insight can lead to aggression and other undesirable and antisocial forms of behaviour that make life difficult for all: children, parents and teachers.

In the exercises we have suggested the children can be led to review a situation or problem. They can be helped to reflect on, and become objective about, their own behaviour. Step by step, working from their own experience, they can learn from that experience. They can develop the flexibility to make necessary adaptations to their actions as situations vary.

Learning about yourself is important. That self, however, is not something which functions in isolation, neither does it develop without other people. The exercises have been selected to help children to learn about others, and so become more tolerant and realistic, and also to learn how to work and play as a member of a group.

The group offers a range of important learning experiences. Every child is born into a group, his family. Research has shown that families differ in the kind of training they offer, and the amount. The learning strategies presented here are models from which the child may learn the skills needed to co-operate with others to achieve an end. He learns to choose, and the exercises can help him see when he decides not to choose, and the feelings which follow his decision. The exercises offer real choices, or remind him of real choices, and bring the question of choice – and so of discipline – to his attention. The growing awareness of discipline will need to be expanded with the teacher's help whenever issues arise in the classroom. Insight gained in the periods given to social and personal education can be stultified if questions and objections are dealt with in an abrupt and authoritarian way at other times. Then the learner would see only more evidence of the unfairness and dishonesty of adults.

The material presented here was chosen to form a bridge; it is not the goal, only a way of moving towards the goal. Exercises have been chosen and designed to give the teacher first-hand experience of humanistic, experiential training. It is hoped that this will lead to a desire to know more, and so the book closes with an annotated list of books and articles which may be of assistance.

Experiencing this form of training yourself is a great help. A structured exercise presented here is just a form of words. Your experience will give it some sort of life as you read, but you will gain much more by trying the activity with a group of children with whom you have a good relationship, and when the time is right. When you have read, experimented and also been a member of a group working in this way, then you will have a rounded experience. No one will need to tell you how important it is to discuss the experience and tie it into other aspects of your life.

This training is available as a short in-service course or a longer course of full- or part-time study at the School of Education, University of Nottingham, where courses in human relations have been running for over a decade. Teachers who have taken part have reported beneficial results in their dealings with children, parents and colleagues. They have found themselves less stressed and better able to deal with stress when it did arise. Discipline improved because they had learned to employ more efficient means of communication, and to deal with problems promptly and openly. Other courses, of varying length, are conducted at the School of Education and Centre for Social and Moral Education, University of Leicester and the Department of Educational Studies, Teesside Polytechnic.

The exercises have been used with a variety of children in primary and secondary schools. Most of these children have been labelled 'difficult' and often 'backward'. All the teachers involved in these trials reported beneficial effects for the children and for themselves. They were all, at some level, students on human-relations courses which offered some training in group and individual counselling skills. Their classroom experience has contributed to the choice of material and the methodology adopted here.

For the purposes of research, the exercises were selected carefully and then used with a group of twelve slow-learning children for one day each week for ten weeks by an experienced and qualified special-education teacher. He made his final choice of exercise, form of presentation, length and format for review in response to his evaluation of the needs of the class – and his own needs – at the time of teaching. Since this is how an experienced teacher operates it is expected that others will use this material in the same way; it is intended to support the practitioner in her exercise of the art of teaching, not to supplant that art.

Over the period of training the children became more friendly. On the measures applied they were shown to be moving closer to one another and to be less inclined to exclude others or hold others at a distance. The friendships built up over this period had been maintained when measured ten weeks after the end of the period. Indeed, friendships had improved and became more stable. An analysis of attendance over the three terms of the year showed that it had become better during the ten weeks of training and remained higher for the term after. The teacher also reported that he found the children more interested in school.

A group of twelve experienced teachers were introduced to these structured exercises and the underlying thinking on a one-week in-service course run by the authors. This was a variation on the well-researched in-service training courses in human relations run at the School of Education, University of Nottingham. It included practice in counselling skills and experience of small-group training, the form of training found most useful and powerful by those who had taken part in it. In a two-day follow-up eight weeks later, most of the teachers reported improved relations with students, and a greater awareness of the strategies they used to relate to others. This awareness was the first stage in deciding what to change, and how to do so. Caution had inclined them to use their new communication skills primarily with other adults, but, having found them effective, they were gradually introducing them into their daily work with the class.

Both groups, the children who helped with the evaluation of the material, and the teachers who attended the one-week course, showed that they could review their established ways of thinking. Having looked carefully at their habitual ways of reacting they could, given a supportive social and physical environment, put up with the discomfort of trying out different and less usual ways of behaviour that they had chosen from the alternatives. It was uncomfortable to explore new ideas, skills and values, and other learners could make it too much to

52

bear if they mocked, derided and opposed change in the would-be innovator. The climate of learning had to be made safe, and increasing the level of friendliness and developing an awareness of the hurtful impact of some forms of automatic defensive behaviour made it safer.

We shall be bearing in mind what these students, teachers and children have told us when we go on to write, adapt and try out further exercises. We hope that their experience will be useful to you too as you try things out. Of course you will be nervous; you would be an insensitive teacher who had not learned from her experience if you were not wary of new approaches. However, if you go slowly and in small steps, watching for the right time, place and group, we feel confident that both you and the children will gain pleasure and benefit from this approach through experience.

Bibliography

References

Amerikaner, M. & Summerlin, M. L. 1982 Group counselling and learning disabled children: effects of social skills and relaxation training on self-concept and classroom behaviours. *J. Learning Disabilities,* **15**(6), 340–344.

Bigelow, B. J. 1977 Children's friendship expectations: a cognitive developmental study. *Child Development,* **48**, 246–253.

Bullock, D. & Severe, S. 1981 Using fantasy and guided visual imagery. *Academic Therapy,* **16**(3), 311–316.

Curwin, R. & Curwin, G. 1974 *Developing Individual Values in the Classroom.* Palo Alto, California: Learning Handbooks.

Goldstein, H. 1974 *Social Learning Curriculum. Phase 8. Getting Along with Others.* Columbus, Ohio: Charles E. Merrill.

Kagan, S. 1985 Co-op co-op: a flexible cooperative learning technique. In *Learning to Cooperate, Cooperating to Learn,* ed. R. Slavin *et al.,* chap. 9. Plenum.

Ladd, G. W. & Emerson, E. S. 1984 Shared knowledge in children's friendships. *Developmental Psychology,* **20**(5), 932–940.

Ladd, G. W. & Mize, J. 1983 A cognitive–social learning model of social-skill training. *Psychological Rev.* **90**(2), 127–157.

McBrien, R. J. 1978 *Using Relaxation Methods with First Grade Boys.* Washington D.C.: American Personal Guidance Association.

Morris, J. 1977 Meditation in the classroom. *Learning,* Dec., pp. 22–27.

Reisman, J. M. & Shorr, S. I. 1978 Friendship claims and expectations among children and adults. *Child Development,* **49**, 913–916.

Rogers, C. R. 1983 *Freedom to Learn for the 80's.* Columbus, Ohio: Charles E. Merrill.

Samuels, S. C. 1977 *Enhancing Self-concept in Early Childhood.* New York: Human Sciences Press.

Selman, R. 1981 The child as a friendship philosopher. In *The Development of Children's Friendships,* ed. S. Asher & J. Gottman, pp. 242–272. Cambridge University Press.

Timmerman, T. & Ballard, J. 1975 *Strategies in Humanistic Education,* vol. 1. Amherst, Massachusetts: Mandala.

Wanat, P. E. 1983 Social skills: an awareness program with learning disabled adolescents. *J. Learning Disabilities,* **16**(1), 35–38.

Research Reports

In-service training at Nottingham

Hall, E., Woodhouse, D. A. & Wooster, A. D. 1984 An evaluation of in-service courses in human relations. *Brit. J. In-Service Education,* **11**(1), 55–60.

Woodhouse, D. A., Hall, E. & Wooster, A. D. 1985*a* Taking control of stress in teaching. *Brit. J. Educational Psychology,* **55**, 119–123.

—— 1985*b* Experiential learning and discipline. *Pastoral Care in Education,* **3**(3), 215–222.

Wooster, A. D., Hall, E. & Woodhouse, D. A. 1986 In-service courses in human relations: one teacher's learning. *Brit. J. Guidance Counselling,* **14**(1), 78–87.

Application in school

Wooster, A. D. 1985 Personal and social development in the primary school. *Pastoral Care in Education,* **3**(3), 183–189.

Wooster, A. D. & Bird, E. G. E. 1979 Meeting pupils: strategies for the pastoral care tutor. *Therapeutic Education,* **7**(2), 44–47.

—— 1980 Social skills training in a pastoral care group. In *Behaviour Problems in the Comprehensive School,* ed. G. Upton & A. Gobell. Faculty of Education, University College, Cardiff.

Wooster, A. D. & Carson, A. 1982 Improving reading and self-concept through communication and social skills training. *Brit. J. Guidance and Counselling,* **10**(1), 83–87.

Research background for this book

Wooster, A. D. & Leech, N. 1985 Personal and social education for slow-learning children: a research and development project. Paper presented at Int. Congr. Special Education, Nottingham, England.

Useful Books and Articles

Adler, R. & Towne, N. 1984 *Looking Out/Looking In: Interpersonal Communication,* 4th edn. Holt, Rienhart & Winston. Gives a large amount of comprehensive information with interesting approaches and exercises.

Aschuler, A. 1980 *School Discipline.* McGraw-Hill. An excellent book that attempts to deal with some of the fundamentals.

Canfield, J. & Wells, H. 1976 *100 Ways to Enhance Self-Concept.* Prentice-Hall. Often regarded as *the* resource book. Many of the exercises are adaptable for slow learners. Expensive.

Cartledge, G. & Milburn, J. (eds) 1980 *Teaching Social Skills to Children.* Pergamon. Gives a thorough account of most of the different approaches to social skills.

Curwin, R. & Curwin, G. 1974 *Developing Individual Values in the Classroom.* Palo Alto, California: Learning Handbooks. A very readable book that gives a usable approach to values clarification.

Curwin, R. & Mendler, A. 1980 *The Discipline Book.* Reston, Virginia: Reston Publishing. Good. Many activities that can be used in the classroom as well as to examine your own view of discipline.

Goldstein, H. 1974 *Social Learning Curriculum.* Columbus, Ohio: Charles E. Merrill. A good series of books giving complete lesson plans with lots of extra information for teaching a very wide range of skills to 'developmentally disadvantaged' children.

Grainger, A. J. 1966 *The Bullring.* Pergamon. The author questions traditional beliefs on 'control' and shows that even where 'chaos' seems to prevail there is an underlying 'order' and learning can take place.

Harmin, M. & Sax, S. 1977 *A Peaceable Classroom.* Minneapolis: Winston Press. Gives lots of activities designed to reduce tensions in the classroom. Includes relaxation, breathing and fantasy.

Hendricks, G. & Roberts, T. B. 1977 *The Second Centering Book.* Prentice-Hall. Follow-up to Hendricks & Wills (1975).

Hendricks, G. & Wills, R. 1975 *The Centering Book.* Prentice-Hall. A readable and well thought-out book with many useful ideas and activities.

Hopson, B. & Scally, M. 1981 *Lifeskills Teaching.* McGraw-Hill. Comprehensive with activities, check-lists and a guide to resources. Includes a section on coping with difficult group members.

Oaklander, V. 1978 *Windows to Our Children.* Moab, Utah: Real People Press. A very readable book that gives lots of moving accounts of the use of fantasy, drawing and other creative techniques with children. Contains many good ideas.

Rose, R. 1980 In *Imagery,* ed. J. E. Storr *et al.*, pp. 281–289. Plenum. This provides a strong argument for the use of guided fantasy and gives suggestions on how to handle opposition from colleagues and parents.

Simon, S. & O'Rourke R. 1977 *Developing Values with Exceptional Children*. Prentice-Hall. Gives strategies and ideas for developing values with children with special needs. Based on work done in a school.

Stevens, J. O. 1971 *Awareness*. Moab, Utah: Real People Press. As well as having plenty of usable material for fantasy and awareness work this book has a very important chapter that gives useful guidelines and warnings for anyone leading a group that is exploring fantasy experience.

Timmerman, T. 1975 *Growing Up Alive*. Amherst, Massachusetts: Mandala. This book gives a large amount of comprehensive information and resource material on humanistic education for children in 'the middle school'. It is backed up with theory.

Wooster, A. & Hall, E. 1985 *Human Relations Training in Schools*. School of Education, University of Nottingham.